A PICAS SERIES BOOK

2000

Signals for Seers

a selection of poems
by

Gilles Hénault

from
Signaux pour les Voyants (1972)
and
À l'Inconnue nue (1984)

translated by

Ray Ellenwood

Exile Editions · Toronto
2000

This edition is published by Exile Editions Limited,
20 Dale Avenue, Toronto, Ontario, Canada   M4W 1K4

SALES DISTRIBUTION:
McArthur & Company
c/o Harper Collins
1995 Markham Road
Toronto, ON
M1B 5M8
toll free:
1 800 387 0117
1 800 668 5788 (fax)

Composed at *MOONS OF JUPITER* Toronto
Cover Collage by *LUDWIG ZELLER*
Printed and Bound by *AGMV MARQUIS*

The publisher wishes to acknowledge
the assistance toward publication of the Canada Council
and the Ontario Arts Council.

ONTARIO ARTS
COUNCIL

CONSEIL DES ARTS
DE L'ONTARIO

THE CANADA COUNCIL | LE CONSEIL DES ARTS
FOR THE ARTS | DU CANADA
SINCE 1957 | DEPUIS 1957

ISBN 1-55096-517-4

Contents

from *Signaux pour les Voyants*

Bordeaux-by-the-Bagnio

1

Words like pebbles of blood in the throat
Words tossed in the face
Hawked up words
Screams erupting from silent stone
dumb flints
suddenly bursting in rocket parabolas
Single spew of hate and love
The whole unspeakable fist thrust up
at a menace teetering
over the heads of the crowd
And international man sprung from the burning mirror
of a working class welded to earth, to hammers, to mines,
to galleries dug in rock salt.

2

The bird of deliverance flutters in the eye of
    convicts
Desires lay rails as far as Sarajevo
where 200,000 picks sing in rhythm.
Revolt must be daily bread
for all those behind bars in Bordeaux-by-the-bagnio
for all those with heels ground down by drudgery
the pissed-off pedestrians
splattered on planetary sidewalks
for all strollers completely out to lunch
for all marchers who talk like they walk
for all appendages to machines with centrifugal hearts
for all who don't speak just to hear themselves talk
but to gripe
at the great nausea of modern times and this unlivable
    world
saying a world upside down is a clawed crab

scuttling backwards into the horror
   of cesspool seas
where all the foetal desires of adolescence
   rot
(blue-blooded rosette)
cesspools for sun flies and cameo rays
cracked trinkets made of starfish with tentacles mounted
on a hypodermic full of serum for tuberculosis
bred by deep-sea viruses ...

And when a man wants to see himself, none of the mirrors
   are silvered.

He'd like to blow it all to hell:
torpor, the streetcar full of flocks steeped in a
   uniform
fatigue of days of fine sand, finks, fists,
the bench, the clock punching out flutterby hours,
overalls smeared with white lead of boredom
the whole shebang!

3

Folk who flock for weeks of lean Maundy Thursdays
and Good Fridays
Mutton heads
Chasuble lovers
Folk asleep at the foot of filthy pulpits
In the land of 25% tithes
With werewolves on the way leading back
to Our Lord l'Histoire
You've come to a crossroad
that separates sheep from wrath
wolf from lamb, pastor from flock,
clown from prop, worker from rack
and the king from a frock
meant to cloak the crossed brooms of a scare-finch,
not to mention his carcass and fetish and minster's crook
and all sorts of priestly trimmings.

4

(And they all sang this song)
Mary had some little lambs
Their fleece was white as snow
And everywhere that Mary went
The lambs were sure to go
But someone fleeced them all one day
On the way to school
Beat them up and made them pay
Selling off their wool
So the lambs turned into wolves
Which was against the rules
And ate up all the bogey-men
Who'd treated them like fools.

1948

Note: The French title, *Bordeaux-sur-bagne,*
refers to the very old Bordeaux prison
in North Montréal.

A Lady of Great Age

Old and gentyle lady
With smile misty as ancient mother sea
Lady of the eye of a lost
palimpsest, gaze lost in the distance, a look older
than the Hypotenuse-Bird's ghost
in the great pyramid
Your glance pours out into shadows void of lightning
Bringing blossoms back to the blue flower
of braided withered years.
Your lineage turns in the noonday sun
Your bygone ages, alternate rose and flame
Your ages engulfed – a tree-top bird
    pecks the ripened fruit of night –
Your ages spreading towards the farthest edge of a
    stele of snow
Your ages tremble returned from afar
since insufficient frost congeals on the lake
to form the ultimate melting shape
adrift in the snow squalls of winter.
Your wrinkles flood into rivers in sleeping shade
Your hair dips long stalactites in tears of the dead
And everything that once was you, your breast
    everything that once was soft, your hand
        everything that once was mad, your serene
palimpsest stare
lost, your errant look propagates it all
With the persistence of webs twenty times renewed
strung after the rain
between boxwood youth and the old age of mistletoe
To catch the dawn.
Everything that once was poison fruit in your mouth
– Belladonna, belle-dame –
Is transforming imperceptibly
into a parasol mushroom, agaric or chanterelle.

1946

To Live Naked

for Captain Bengoose

To live naked on the beach of time!
Let sand run ceaseless
in the hourglass of the sea!
Can't you tell sea shells
are aquatic telephones?
The wave I straddle is a young colt.
His horseshoes strike a pebble sound
His mane muffles his cry
His white mane
is an avalanche of salt
And his flanks
rock the sky in this see-saw landscape.
Soon the wind will toss me beyond the madding crowd.
Memories die in oblivion's wake
While rising sharks nibble
    the foolish fish of April first!
The sea friend and mistress
Picks the lock of seasons
Where wind teases sail.
Oh, life is a journey
And time foams along the hull.
Sea frees me from the clockwork
Steps of measured earth.
The sailor's soul is phosphorescent
From peering at so many beacons
with their drowned arms outstretched in the fog.
Surely islands call me?
My soul shifts with the winds.
Was ever a mariner more alive
than when his life is a waltz
from one land's end to another?
The glaciers of my dreams drift south
Bound for the Gulf Stream's source
Where creole smiles
And salt flats
And the song of lyre-birds gleam.
To live naked on the sands of time
For freedom is spring tide
And the sky mirrors solitude.

   1946

Open Air Theatre

Night flows in my nerves. The murmur grows impatient beating tympana with muffled, heavy strokes, velvet taut over trap drums, tom-tom frantic against an overturned sky letting a hundred million stars rain down.

The theatre has no walls. Four seasons make a silent cloister: snow, rain, frost and soot cornered by the winds of March and April.

Phantom actors play at believing they're alive. What a wordless, tearless puppet show. And among all these people (speech-makers turned shapers of silence whose mispronounced words fly off like wounded fowl) the conjurer finds and loses himself again and again, convinced he's a bird-catcher.

Night with no beacon and ship without sail: all is silence, a flow of vague wavings and soundless surf. Perched on the topmost branch of night, the ether sleeps. And yet, many signs over the sea. Stars are water lilies.

Old mysteries and young marvels ask each other whispered questions in the wings, so dogs bark at the moon. They look around and sniff the approach of unknown persons they could never bite.

Sleeping men assign parts in their dreams and characters shred their scattered souls like a pack of hounds. They alone people the night.

Simultaneously, two soul-sisters receive passports for lands found at the antipodes. As far as catastrophes go, this must be the worst! The anguished question is asked: what force will reunite these torn and divergent souls? Never was a man so showered with insults as these two women in love with a single body; never was a seraglio so divided against itself.

Ah! So many faithless and stupid thoughts shout on the stages of sleep. And yet death is not far off. Of course I spot it in that spider spinning a web of effects and causes on the clearly illusory ceiling.

But the set and actors change. Main character: light.

1946

Portrait of a Balinese

Black palm grove silence
Mirrors its spears in your face
Oh distant, and yet so near
Sister. Heart of the well-springs of dream
Oh Balinese woman deep in lustral waters of space
Which rock and maintain the flame of your image – magic
The frantic dreams of your race float down
    the course of your carnal growth.
Rhythmic dugouts drift
dugouts drift on the newsprung wave
    rolling again for the thousand thousandth time
To come undone in the play of your swinging hips.
And you cannot stop your closed mouth from singing
    the songs of your people
Songs no alalia can silence.
Ah! whisper that weaves a weft for the high
    clear light of the islands.
Are you smiling still on the shore of time
    as it tilts towards your dream
Oh you, singular in form
    and the only woman
Poised in air outlined by your arms
And the only intelligent being bending its head over the shadow
    of your neck.
– Fresher fold in the less cool wave –
By the grace of your slender fingers you rise
    above the sea
    above the bittersea human race.
Such is the vigor of silence and stillness
Such is the taste of the great kiss of shadow on your skin
Such is the salt of your glance that it lights sagacious sparks
    in full sunlight
Among lofty winged victories.

1946

The Traveller

He's running, he's running, he'll never arrive. The train gone, the boat sunk, the plane only a shadowy cross over wheat fields.

He's walking, he's walking, Monday, Tuesday, Wednesday the whole week. Ah! maybe the motel will fly away.

But there's this eternally motionless clock staring at time through mechanical eyes.

He's running, running, towards the station's phosphorescent clock.

But there's this stupid dead-end street in mid-air. Endless space opens, the eye turns and reads, never stopping: attention, the train is leaving the station ... attention, the train is leaving the station, attention ...

Enough! enough! Seasons change, years go by, rivers flow, the earth's too small, through some mysterious magic spell day and night swell the same space, when all of a sudden we see a lamp looming out of this nightmare.

Its light alone fills the void while day and night divide the poles between them.

He's running, running, he'll never arrive.

The earth is turning backwards. He's a trained dog in a spinning wheel. He's a clown on a ball in mid-bazaar as a brawl settles over the city.

No, it's not so bad, he's just walking. They thought he was running because he's old and he's got the shakes.

Exhausted is hardly the word, crushed under an archangel's heel: that's the truth of the matter.

While the sun at last rises, and while swamps smoke fanned by a south wind, he stops, full of the airsick vomit of voracious vultures, balanced on the end of the world, dipping a toe in shit.

He's arrived, but doesn't know where. Of course, it's a boneyard for elephants and for once the dawn comes up in the West.

Only a boring word could describe this show – well I'll be damned, he says, maybe the sun's left-handed!

1946

Comrades

Well, comrades
what have you got in your hearts?
A song, a little common sense,
revolution?
So tell me comrades,
tell me, what have you got?
Lead fatigue scuttles your legs
this trek is not too tough
Ah! but the earth is round.
What do you hear by night comrades
by night, comrades, by night?
It's the immense marching stride
the climb, the rising tide
the trembling earth terrified
Enemy signals drumming on the moon
The ant-hill gutted
It's China snared in the spider's web
of your studied stratagems
and ricefields reflecting eyes asquint with fear
It's Greece blown up like a star.
Wheat sprouts rampant on the ramparts
Ploughshares strike bayonets
It's warfare buried forever ...

*

Ah! comrade
can't you see the city grow
the city bearing fruit
Flinging its gates open to armies of the dawn!
Can't you see that love
at last is a simple act reconciling
two breathing bodies
to one rhythm
no more obscene
than sowing
no more strange
than a blade of grass
no more dumb
than words

no more galling
than a western gale
no more deadly
than the sun rising.
Ah! the body restored at last to wholeness
In the act of swimming man utters
his greatest metamorphoses
Woman bends tighter than a bow
Her whole body saying one single
unspeakable word.

1948

Short Apocryphal Genesis

to Roland Giguère

1

Adam and Eve
mere mirages
at time's wellspring.

2

Eve of the virginal
teeth
Eve and Adam
discover pollen.
Adam and Eve of the virginal lips
plant the tree of humankind.

3

Acephalous woman
Fertile Venus
Where mankind takes root
Breasts, womb, vagina
Cycle of love and clay
Woman, part shadow
Both feet in earth
And arms in the sky
You are the horizon of our childhood
And you blaze in the sun
Of our carnal love.

4

A life sacrificed
to the tip of its stem
A beautiful pruned tree of life
Bends the fruit of its breasts
Down to proliferating generations
So its slavery
May give survivors
A sweet calm shade.

5

An Eden of breadbearing trees and lost time
Mingled with sand
Stars caught in nets
Were playing will-o'-the-wisp
It was in the age of thornless love
Of youth in bloom
Of women without paint
And men without memory.

6

On that day
God appeared in all His glory:
In a violet robe
with white buttons
his bluish beard
his hair undulating with lightning
He lit a menorah
and lo there was light!
Adam straddling the horizon
Between oceans of Good and Evil
Awaited the signal to dive.
Satan was napping
On the beach of time.

7

The horse invented his breed
with mane and canter
He invented rhythm and leaping
But already dreamt of foreign roots
Of whips, ploughs, work and war
Because mankind ...
Had eaten the apple.

8

God put on his policeman's suit
His triple-striped cap
Sheathed his sword
A stony heart beneath his tunic
And set off for earth
Followed by the archangel, his adjutant
Father going to punish the children

Because of a sour apple
Adam had eaten
God guarded his orchard
For, though he loves mankind
his children
He loves apple jelly
Even more.

9

Then we knew
Seasons of savage beasts
We warred against
Half-human monsters
We invented
Dazzling reason
We discovered
The cock and his song
We straddled
The aurochs and bison
We lit
the fire of hope
in the depths of our hearts.
And one fine morning, the sun rose
to the cock's crow!

10

Mankind left behind the night of prehistory
The age of stone and wood-louse
At cave mouth
He planted the totem of his destiny
Camels invented caravans
And mankind knew mirages
age after age
In a desert of thirst and sand
and insatiable desires.

11

And yet oases
reflect a palm-treed future
in the inner sky of every man
who sees others as his brothers
and sees peace as quenching water.

12

Totem your shadow
declines at noon
The earth sways
its generous hips
Rivers rock
in the cradle of their beds
Harvests swoon
as the breeze combs them
The child opens eyes
wide as hands
He begins the game
of loving love, life, bread
And the rose of winds
augurs fair weather.

1953

Childhood

Inside my head is bright with snowbeams.
Wolves stalk Christmases past.
By gong and knell lashed by blizzard
I conjure a childhood of castles in Spain
Vitriol of blue years
Sweetness of hemp-fingered fire
Tapers and tinny flutes
Of the tired song of yesteryear
Barrel-organ of dying civilizations.

The world ebbs like the tide
While we think more and see less.

1953

A Song of Cigarette Butts

1

She's gone leaving her butts behind.
Hey! why not, fire tells no tales
And the art of elegant smoking graces the world.
How say you, hobgoblins of our magic days?
Such times are fled as the soul cries out for
a bloom of dangerous journeys.

2

She's gone leaving her butts behind.
The flight of a sleek sail is transparent
across remembered horizons
where an oar wrecks the waves of dream forever.
She left without her cherry-heart goldfish
Without the rays of rainless days
without the mantle of noise woven by passing trains
without the little red riding hood of fleeting suns
without the teddy bear sitting in a downpour's desolation.

3

She's gone frontside back
her youth unravelled
leaving poison like a fruit.
No knife cuts like a burst of laughter
The contorted face is a bright, bright screen
On the first day, she made a spring flow from her hair
Never forget it
The second was a day of cloudless love on summer's isles
And the others were caravan-days
The orient paled beside this two-headed beast
And on the last day she went
leaving her butts
leaving her fan of puzzling pranks
a lock of her hair on the latch
her fingerprints on the ceiling
her exploded fits of rage
through which the winds of future years now blow.

1953

Hail to Thee

1

Redskins
Tribes lost
in the conflagration of consumption and fire-water
Hunted down by the pallor of death and Palefaces
Carrying dreams of ancestral spirits and manitou
Dreams shattered by musket fire
You left a legacy of totemic hopes
And now our sky is the color
of smoking peace pipes.

2

We've no boundaries
Abundance is our mother.
Steel-belted country
With great lakes for eyes
And a rustling resinous beard
Hail to thee and your waterfalls of laughter
Country capped by polar ice
Beneath a boreal halo
Offering generations to come
A sparkling wreath of uranium fires.
As for those who ransack and drain you
grown fat on your huge body of humus and snow
We thunder them with curses out of the throats of storms.

3

I can already hear the song of those who sing:
Hail to thee, life full of grace
the sower is with thee
blessed art thou through all women
and the child delirious with discovery
holds you in his hand
like the rainbow pebble of reality.

Lovely life, mother of our eyes
clothed in rain and fair weather
may thy kingdom come
thy will be done on roads and fields
Beautiful life
Long live love and spring.

1953

Bestiary

One cry

grunting, hooting, mewling, bleating, barking, neighing, yelping, hissing, roaring,

one cry

is enough for an animal, one visceral cry, a single surge of his whole being, one cry modulating as his instinct meanders, the shimmer of his coat, the intensity of his rage, biological images cracked and crazed, fear and trembling,

one cry

and his tribe pricks its ears, wings thrash, backs rear up, hooves drum on the plains, the charge is headlong, panic makes a lemming-rush to the sea,

one cry

is a call to combat for males humped round the magnet of rut, a homing in on springs that shine in the nostrils of dominant bulls, the immemorial trek to the boneyard where the elephant trumpets his last.

But we are mute.

We must find the cry that will rouse every fear, express every joy, make man speak to man from the guts at last and from his most secret lusts.

The articulate word dries as it branches. Too much ornament hides the secret sense of words, too many flowers of rhetoric weave plastic wreaths for our most naked feelings. I need words stripped to the bone.

I need words like bullets, pure piercing cries. Poetry wants to rock the soul to sleep when it should maul things and cause the naked cry of man to be heard affirming his unique and gregarious existence over the strident voices of religion, philosophy, ethics and politics.

Ah, let the rotten fruit of despair drop at last; let fake enchantments fall on the sharpest thorns; let panic strike the idea fixed far in the starry depths of our skulls; let cataclysms grow tame; let joy spatter us with its blood, even at the risk of death.

We are not done taking stock of the world. To hell with the wind of spirit as long as real mineral torments blow in my face and grit from Sahara and Gobi grinds in my teeth; as long as I feel the enormous breath of sea storms, full of salt and seaweed, oh tears drowned in the backwash when warships are boarded. The whole sea mutinies and cracks the frozen flag of polar ice. The soul's motion is the motion of waves. And when I suddenly feel sheer scope overwhelm me, my veins become the rivers of the world, for my body is the tide, I am washed in the universal lymph, the fibres of my being are immersed in the flow of physical time and I am porous.

I want to lower every defense, burn every prohibition, strip all those who for centuries have strutted in the wraps of wisdom, prophesying on the strength of their gaudy plumage.

I want to chip away at all the gods, demigods and semigods until there's nothing left but a tiny heap of slag.

I want my anger turned to stones in my fists.

1959

Rocket

At first it was just a crackling of sparks at the edge of the lash. The eye's iris bloomed deep in the night. Of course we knew comets passed this way, leaving wakes of aurora borealis. But there was no warning morning would split so brightly.

The earth opened wide, exposing geological ages from the dawn of time; planets in embryo; sketchy skeletons; paltry scaffolding rising in tiers to an epidermis of chlorophyll which for so long has given it that tinge of an ailing star.

The tick-tock of uranium was heard in the four corners of space-time, playing counterpoint to pulsing tides. We'd grown accustomed to those syncopated rhythms, to that staccato unfolding of the cosmic clock.

And yet nuclear terror grew in poison mushrooms, and yet panic seized electrons at the heart of minerals, and yet the tree of generations gave only contaminated fruit, ripe before birth, floating like May flies on the temporal flood and gliding on the flank of falling gamma rays towards a crackling void.

And that was when we heard the cataract crumble, that choric whinny of all the horses in the world, and saw the horizon slice from its sequent the stem of a withered sun.

A distress rocket soared to the zenith, taking the only rose left in our garden of illusions!

Oh what kind of rudderless drift has carried us into this calm of a nebula among spooked compasses. The bent gyroscope will go on fooling us as we move through the skies, pursuing a light that is fleeting ... fleeting ...

I remember soil nourished with alluvium where soothed eyes could read nothing but herbaceous youth. I remember a sea eternally new at the cutwater of a continent, its islands capped by trees and birds. But what good are sedimentary regrets, the veined joys of multicolored cries in a stratified past?

I try to imagine the humblest, sweetest, most moving thing in the world. Hybrid petals suddenly grow, crystals of flame swimming on feathered suns, drops of water colored with salt on the pearly deep of memory.

I do believe we used to call it the look in a woman's eye as diamond-cutting love shaped its facets.

1959

The Game of Love

The night sang its quiet treefrog mating song, braiding its locks of sinuous reeds. Evanescent cries traced prophetic curves, tracking night birds.

And my desire made its nest in the tree of your veins.

A river flowed over you, bridged by a great tremble of milky way where the constellation of your sex and breasts glowed, stars full-blown waterlilies on the long stem of a gaze.

Deeper than waters sheltering moon trout, more secret than the dream of a terraced wave in the sky's mirage, you broadcast your silence beyond the zone where I stood. Silence stirred the womb of speech, aeolian ovaries conceived the storm of a lightning-rumpled passion.

And my desire cried aloud in the tree of your veins.

The great shadowed motion of eclipse foretold a close conjunction of eyes, a confluence of fevers on the banks of our lips and the gush of a diamond-sharp ahh scoring the silence – a star-shaped incision of bursting laughter.

Silence lies becalmed. Thus the water's wound is healed behind the diving moon-trout. Thus chaste waters slip off their sheen, thus a fluttering eyelid returns to headwaters of memory. Thus flame becomes woman.

Sooner die than never swim for such star-studded shores of promised joy. We were out in the great maternal night, with the heaving breath of wind and murmur of crickets around us, with the soft hiss of grasses whispering growth while rivers in rut ravished the sea and the tides' ebb and flow rocked a troubled world under the turning eye of beacons.

And my desire sang in the tree of your veins.

It sang so well, I made a midnight sun rise in your eye and for you I invented a whole cosmos of ritual signs and syllables blooming like stars in the microcosm of our love.

1959

The Ark

They've been cooped in a sort of Noah's ark,
surrounded by lunar snow, stern Jansenist
icicles, slag heaps piled high as cathedrals
and a host of raw knees on cold planks.
Lamp and larynx breathe smoky prayers.

The ark's walls are festooned with foetuses and empty shells,
with eyes glued to genitals, with the black, cruel plumage of
birds of exorcism. The sour saltpetre of spleen sweats through
chinks of stony hours. A strange baboon language is spoken
here, mottled by gestures, incense and ringing bells of despair.

In every nook of these aquarium corridors, children
smother their cries. They stare like dead fish.
Spider webs are signboards of sin. Everywhere defenses
raise stockades, revolt hides in shadows cast by bars,
all desire is straitjacketed.

Apparently, this is how elites are made.

1960

The Great Sacristans

Nothing is so unsettling
as these fluid times
days between ebb and flood
lights that flare and flicker
and flare again in the fresh wind.

Nothing is so unsettling
as these ferocious faces
blood-bath heads and hangmen
whose rotten teeth bite the flesh
of a young, clear-eyed future.

These loose lips curled
around arthritic lies
these wounded words misguiding the flight of speech
these hands clutching gold that rings like gunmetal
these monsters who go to the ball ... masked.

.

Known world barbaric world
reflected in pools of blood
world where Great Sacristans
stand guard armed with extinguishers.

Extinguishers for everything: pangs of conscience
good deeds, fires of knowledge
the tiny rekindling embers of hope
great flashing petroleum passions
the furnace of justice in a crowd's heart
sunset blaze over harvests of peace.

World of sheer concrete walls
world of padded cells
world of caparisoned carcasses
world of decorated monsters
free world in gilded chains
infernal world that's lived too long.

Black, yellow, red continents
bare their millennial stigmata

and straighten aching old backs
their heads rise above rice fields and jungles
and the lovely dreams they see are nightmares
in the oxidized eyes of the occident.

1961

Semaphore

1

Signs drift into silence
Signs drift into sands of dream and disappear
Signs seep through the pupil's inverted sky
Signs crackle, radiations of noxious essence
chemistry of kinetic forms, filigranes of aurora
borealis.
And all spun from leafy memories, palmate gestures
fanning the space of smooth jubilation.
Signs are roots, spreading stalks, sprouting signals
as the wind leafs through its book of spells.
It is winter and the land puts on its seamless robe
with a grand flight of leaves and feathers, with a sorcerer's sweep
saluting a last gasp of flame.
Under the arching sky
a salt squall flares
Sign of a silence which gushes from dream and spleen
Silence lances the landscape's heart
suddenly whipped by violent gusts and the storm comes up like a
froth of legend staining the signet rings of night.
The man midstream in age no longer knows
what shore his life is coming from

2

Signs, silence, smoke
Deserted dream, blank page
Sphere suddenly full of curdled solitude
like ivory asterisks swirling in glass balls
Moment of utter nudity under the halo of streetlamps
lone signs of human warmth in the distance
That howling is just the voice of dogs long dead
as the snapping wind rouses a pack
of long years squandered day by day
forlorn gestures
Mobility ices over and the span, the span of time congeals
on the lake of memory

3

Signs into silence
Silence scattered down snow-bound litanies
Cold sowed along wind-swept roads
where man loses track of himself, his steps mocked

caught in swirling snares
for even remembrance of fire falters and the future
is studded with ephemera
Drink and delight are eunuch's yearnings
when the core of the present is ringed by terror
Vertical, life devoids itself

4

Snow lashes the face leaning towards the last stubborn
leaf of autumn
towards the tenderness of purple dusk
towards sylvan incense running the length
of resinous summers
Towards the tiny piercing joy of the last bird's song
Icy call, frozen fountain, prism of plundered melody
The hobnailed sound of the wind shatters reverie
Signals, faded dreams
Cold slowly tunnels through the wretched snowman
till he's full of holes
a sonorous cave bristling with stalactites

5

Signals sent from a living sea, what's become of you?
The whole land is bathed in vague melancholy
Fake virgin, faithless vestal
the storm rips her washerwoman's clothes
on the peaks of the Rockies
Storm, wild storm, cast yourself in the sea
where waves utter crazed incantations
The man in his snow conch hears them roar
They tell such fine tales of aliferous infancy
he doesn't know if the sea is beating its wings
or if memory is finally cracking the cold spell's door

6

Sovereign sign
The clock strikes the pearly hour of winter solstice
And since time is congealing
it's no use watching sinuous wreaths
of blizzard unravel
The seer's cropped contemplation drains

like honeycomb
In his cold alveolus a man dreams of summer nectar
His face hung out like a sheet to the sting of snow bees
swarming images
Sleep is dough for his bread
Impaled on an icicle of austere expectation
he dares not move
Partitioned
an ice leaf separates him from death
translucent leaf, stained glass prefiguring
pale arabesques of absence
Ill-fated signs
first glimmerings from beyond the dream

7

And yet we had filled our holds with sprightly friendships
of flint. What ever became of the sparks – cold
stones, flint bereft of fire, wounding arrowheads – Nothing
cuts like carefully honed hate, except perhaps
crystals of silence. In any other season love survives
like sisal or avocado under large white and
blue panes of veiled glances. But nothing grows
under cold's arcade, beneath winter's palm even rivers
are frozen in their beds.

8

Sign of abandon
In winter's fief, usufructs are scattered to the winds
Nothing falls to the lot of common souls
but a swarm of evanescent sequins
The rose window of wonder comes alive
for those who can see a crystal theophany dancing in air
The luckiest signs seem arcane
to snuffed eyes
But the guileless soul stamps its effigy on all things
Ah, the sudden flare of laughter on welcoming slopes!
In the curvature of space, light unfurls its chrysalis
Its moist wing covers the morning tree
A washday wind blows West to East
scent of clean laundry

rustle of flags frozen to the pole of vertigo
The landscape, varnished with verglas,
covered with ideograms, is unliveable
except perhaps in the ring of light cast by a lover's eye

9

Signs stripped to acronyms
What paleographer can read bare tundra?
Wandering wolves howl and howl at the moon
trying to decode the great ice alphabet
Hunger cold windswept words lighter than drifting chaff
all the sweetness of life has been sifted through forest screens
That is when love curls up in the palms of glittering houses
At daybreak a couple leans over a future
of gardens
certified by the last twig

10

Sign of errant death
Time wipes the slate
Yesterday is a closed door
The wind repeats the same ashen phrase
The same sooty words
Alphabet of cold coals
of burnt-out joys like fireflies drowned
in darkest summer
Icicles gently probe the heart
blood carries silt down to the bitter dead season
It is snowing mean little needles on a landscape
barbed by wire
Space expands to fill the cold

11

Billow blizzard blackness
the word for birth freezes in the mouth
a man lies with his soul stripped under opaque days
But a slab lifts in the stream of becoming
a dawn slab risen for the resurrection of sap
for the metamorphosis of dreams into digital signs.
The flood loosens the tongue

Signs and spells
The woman waves oriflammes between lamp and bed
And a swung hip forecasts high tide
in coves of flesh
Figurehead woman, prowess, casts off love's moorings
and launches a flight of gulls to greet her male
Hand signals
flight of feathered words gliding straight to the heart
Collapse of enigmas
Distance disappears in the light of desire, warmth
seeps into snow-bound chambers, raging rivers suddenly bawl
loud songs of liberation, a torrent bears on its
croup the passion of waves and it is time
for the great insurrection of sap.
Ice, mirrors, everything cracks and blends
The harnessed river rears at the bridling dam
and like an army breaking its spears in sunlight
the season shines in the sign of the Ram.

.

Leaves explode like firedamp
What will become of us, peppered by pollen shot?

1962

Assassination

The Marquise met her death
screaming: 'Save my diamonds!'

Down, down with
the virus, the cancer, the false coin of helpless screams
Down, down with lampshades of memory
false joys, false reckonings, false collars
false incursions
of men in search of their navels.
Long live the dagger's point!
Diamonds no longer scream in the night
The miner is mined
But the hymen glows with a violet flame
The miner is minimal
And little black boy hungry
Little black boy thirsty.
The diamond screams revenge to the earth's four corners
Exploding ...
The diamond burns masking the pallor of pale faces
Opens its fan of red corpuscles
Its aurora borealis thunders distant mutinies
The diamond lowers its antennae
The green beam opens artillery fire
on a peerless carnival.

How come the Marquise is made of wax, you might ask
Very simple, it was raining
that night
but daggers do not melt.

1962

Here Comes the Time

1

I'm someone who accepts
The light and night of our paltry years
One of those who read
The shadows of our hands cast upon coming actions
I'm one who speaks
With his mouth full of bitter certainty
One of those who see
Spells of the earth in the eyes of women
I'm one who combs
The tails of comets
One of those who know
That miracles are made of men
Because I've picked my loveliest flowers in the frost
Flowers of lucid reason
Which trap light.

2

Here comes the time of clear sight
    and new beauties
After the hell of metamorphoses.
Salt of the earth will cover winter's wounds
Peace will pour floods
On the ash of our burnt-out hopes
A bleeding human harvest will no longer
    bend over mirrors of sky
And the devil's hide will dry in the four winds
Like a scarecrow.

1962

Time Like a Tree

1

Blank sleepless night brushed on the wall of sound
A single laugh can crack you
And despite this frost branched through
with the mundane irony of survival
Despite this vein of shadow where blood is no longer current
Life beats in the heart of winter
Distilling her wide puddles of petroleum
Spouting spongy words through all her pores
Gushing petrified wells to form menhirs.
Now is the time of accommodation
    to slow gestures of alcohol
Avoiding a skid into night.
Vertigo light photons with colored waves
Swarm of signs
Insect writing
Rustling of seconds
What sort of sand is sifting on the tray of time!
Endlessly engaged making moulds of misfortune
We tangle the lines of chance
Written on the palm of the landscape.

2

Familiar paths hold us in their seine
Millennia of trees wound the bled sky
Roots mute words, roots
Hundreds of millions of times repeated full in the earth
Muffled dialogue with the flat silence of the plain
Have we therefore forgotten the clamorous roads
    of the sea
And its billions of pebbles prating at the lips
    of beaches!
Round words, polished words, thundering words
Whistling words in the slings of breaking crests
May you roll at last to the sonorous fountains
To percussive memories
To the headwaters of the poem.

3

Between veins of trees and veins of men
Telluric saps flow
I read the forest's

Totemic tattoos
Barks papyrus palimpsests
Hieroglyphic monuments
Time is taking root
Branching out and shredding our days
Filling naked space with our quietude.

1962

You Exorcise Me

Put your hand on my brow
so once again I'll have a hint of what life's like
as it opens its petals.
Your hand masks mortality
Your eyes are the color of happiness
Your smile
    break-up of bound horizons
opens a road in spring flood for me
Your words loose crazed horses
whose foam blends with the red wind of my blood
Put your hand on my brow
So once again I'll know what the word presence means.

Islands the color of orange and summer
Islands I cross going to you on the ark of confidence.
Hand cast the moorings
Who cares if a fang strikes the heart
I'll read your traces in sand
Hand you populate the world
and through you I know the present is not
    the stuff of illusion
and I could roll myself in it to sleep
as in a hammock hung outside of time
with a still landscape all around.
Nude thoughts bathe in your eyes
I recognize their algae and coral shapes
their transparency like blind luminous fish.

Cool webbed hand of rivers, fluid joy, vast and
sonorous day, slow snow over calcination of hours
You alone have this power
to thaw absence
to shape the contours of mineral day
to bend light towards the planet where I exile myself
to escape the gyrations of useless gesture.

    1962

I Seek Advice

All the gold you could covet ripens in autumn trees
More profligate with their coin than counterfeiters
Filigranes of leaves signatures of a translucent future
If time sheds its leaves the day will brighten
Have pity on light have pity
Paltry recourse to trees and birds
To the word love that bubble of air
To all things that glitter as a setting for the season
of man.

I seek advice on stone
Where the wind's door swings.

Time turns to a skeleton
Space bares its bones and becomes daylight
The season spreads its membraneous wing
And drifts towards snowlight.
Everything occurs at a distance
The trees are now no more than fusing frozen cries
What are the fruits we should reach for when time is shedding
    its leaves?

I seek advice on stone
Where a vein of light self-immolates.

You used to say life can be tamed you said
That spring would braid its hair into summer's dreams
That threads of joy would stretch from birdsong to bough.

And yet all is fled into links of lightning
And here we are in this trompe-l'oeil landscape
Where everything is distant
In the heartland of shadowless objects signs without substance
Semaphores of a promise bound for perdition.

1962

The Neurotic Dog

1

The neurotic dog
paces within sheer walls of opaque fear
Insomnia has emptied his eyes
He's lost sight of his little bitch
his little bitch of a life who's sitting up pretty
with her handsome new collar that chokes
and a spliced leash
dragging a biped instead of a kennel

2

The neurotic dog hasn't slept
He barks silently all night long
He's digging a tunnel towards a dawn
    bleached as bone
He chews rags, cardboard, pebbles
He's exhausted from playing dumb animal
His nerves are dead roots, rootlets
He feels trussed like a sausage
Leaps and bounds bounce in his body
– putrid water, sluggish petrol –
His memory delves in vain
for puddles of milk, caresses, glutted ease
finding nothing but nights of quick lime
the deep blood of wounds
the crevasses of empty and snow-filled days.

The neurotic dog is still
His instinct an odorless flower in a
    mineral landscape
The paths of his reflex are drained of color
A lone desiccated tree stands there
A lone tree shaped like anguish
His life is petrified geography
Porcupine quills sprout from him
His muzzle stretches towards scattered tracks
eaten by acid, covered with yellowed leaves
tracks promising monstrous images
of howls locked inside wells within walls

3

The neurotic dog
Sniffs at the doors of sealed rooms
– years of mildew
– poison mushrooms
– his little bitch of a life
– his little bitch sitting up pretty
hung by her handsome collar
on the wall of an endless gallery of ancient gestures
– ossuary of dry days and tarnished joys.
The neurotic dog
will bite his little bitch of a life
dragging a biped
built like a kennel on piles.

1962

To the Memory of Paul Eluard

Hands held out to the fire to flowers
To gentle birds signalling peace
To the animals in your landscapes
Hands held out to mankind.
You guide our steps

Hands brewing night
Hands full of serene dawn
Hands helping to see
The world as it's made for us

You undress light itself

Hands hills and miracles
Wonder of eyes wedded to the world
And fertile with promise of joy

Paul Eluard

Your hand holds out to us
our gleedom.

1962

from *A l'Inconnue nue*

To the Unknown Nude VI

When you're far away I invent you out of nothing: breasts,
bellies, some shoulders bending over constellations of thighs
that slip towards a sea of kisses of sand sun eye and mute mouth
of ears deaf shells or hair with frantic waves violent wind of
southern music. Nowhere are you complete and entirely yourself
except – perhaps – in the seaweed sheets of an innocent love.

Your body is my port – your love my star.

You alone I love and will love in all latitudes all
guises. You are my wine (which is not to be sneered at).

In vain you'd like me to come about, capsize, change tack
... but the old captain's set his cap by you: navigation
(countless sirens) divagation (countless tricks) everything makes
way as I quest for your fleece, and for you (idle-winged omens of
shipwreck).

I sail I sail young male ...

(It aint so easy old wheezer.)

1984

To the Unknown Nude XI

Solitude: blank screen ...

My movie comes to life everything goes green the toads croak
Moroccan night ... The wind builds divans on the beach (story of
eau) bodies wet with Koranic prayers ... sailing veils on the
face of the sea ... beautiful body wave body the tide rises up
to the sand asleep in the dry ... ebb-tide tosses back in
the sea a whole cavalry of pebbles ... our damp salty soused
bodies draw back ... crabs sated in the midst of night.

The come (not in Webster's) filled her mouth and so
thanks be to Holy Mother Church we avoid abortion ... the
breeze blessed us ... spindrift of Koran the sea mother of all
life threw her immense tidal laughter far away ... so
everything may begin again ...

1984

To the Unknown Nude XII

Between us a taut wire ...

    A funambulist perambulates there ... his misty eyes see
only your body ... I hear only your body (a tiny cry between
your thighs) your soul swings on a trapeze – circus of my
nights.

– Take the bull by the horns ... bronzed bullfighter defeats
death
– ready the lioness roaring for love of you ...
(tiny little man)
– straddle the doe while the horse bucks ...
Circus: women coiled in acrobatic vertigo ...
a flight of fancy tricks ... falling stars on the
tent's roof ... nets ...

    This distance between us despite our clasped wrists ... (so
the conjugation of sex is no longer a grammatical question?)

It's true you're the Unknown Nude (nudity symbolizes nothing but
birth or death).

    On the high wire I tell tall tales ... my balance
is uncertain ... even more than your unknowable
look (uncatchable?)

    1984

To the Unknown Nude XIV

Because you are naked I believe you

Words (bulls as the Popes used to say!) offered
unadorned: your whole body speaks as your mouth.
It's a miracle we beautiful beasts can talk!

Your hand fittingly gloved with desire makes me moan ... I
nest in the estuary to which the flight of my words has carried
me: migration of sheer strength plumed with sunbeams ...

(To rejoice at being a philosopher and knowing the orgasm
of contradiction in our different yet similar beings.)

A man will never, never understand how a woman comes:
only reads her (indecipherable poem) feeling the wave that
carries her in tune with the tide carrying him ... Navigation:
changing tack in the confines of love ... sudden leeward swing
of the wind's delirious head of sail ... beachings in azure and
resin gulfs ...

And there dear unknown nude you have my definition
(redundant) of sensuality ...

(The main sail's dead ... lower the jib.)

1984

To the Unknown Nude XVI

It's you I speak to whoever you are ...

My tongue is on your sex and I say the most beautiful
clitoridian words (language of Eros) vibratile words of warmth:
this language constructs you inserts you in my universe of liquid
joy.

Water always erodes rock in the end: if my meanderings
take me to death they do so slowly and on the way they mirror
tree-silence cub-ursus sea urchin ... every bird in the sky
swims there while fish fly to branches of mirage ... Thus we're
embroiled in that great failed running aground where even nature
can't conceive of birth and death: the essence and appearance.

I'm telling you things that don't make sense because my
senses are tongue-tied ... it would be wrong to catalogue you:
breasts ... belly ... vagina ... buttocks ... thighs ... calfs
because from head to toe by way of the groin (estuary) of
hair at the curve of loin you are river you are ever-changing
undulation ...

(*One can never bathe in the same river twice*) old
Heraclitus used to say.

1984

To the Unknown Nude XVII

Nudity   all the old myths come to cover you with
their shadow ... sprinkled with holy water sex floats on
detergent litanies ...

   Unveiling your body you have set the table for great
venisons of desire – space where freshly uncorked gallops of
champagne snort – when the party capsizes into bubbling eyes ...
monsoon of phantoms ... harvest of herbaceous riches hugging
the soil: fragrances colors odors of flowers fading as they go
bouquet of earthly sustenance violently offered to all the
senses.

   What I integrate with nudity is the geography of every
pleasure a territory at last for the most carnal venery ...
from that I foresee an era of great spiritual hunts for an eye
lighting the night with its life-assertive assent. (Whoever says
yes does so with the entire body otherwise it means nothing)

   1984

To the Unknown Nude XXII

'Alas, the flesh is forlorn and I've read all the
books,' he said ...

Flee towards a *'suicide beau'* ... better to
take a drunken boat and drift in the direction of all the pores
all the corporeal vessels rocking in coves ... libraries
liberate only small parts of their secrets ... the same with
women ...

Always flip through read newfound delirium reread rewrite
the text discover horizons of words never said ...

The couple sprouts feathers and wonders about its birth
its journey ... migrations plural desires of wild geese ...
wild desires of snow geese (girl I hope you understand me) desire
of the woman plumes him to desire for wings the better to know
the span of the world ...

I plunge into myself like a magic gull searching for what
makes me live ... I emerge from wine-dark mother sea with a
child in my arms: this dream (and it is one) shoves me back to
the shores of a woman flipping through a book of sated flesh –
vitality.

1984

To the Unknown Nude XXIV

Don't leave me little body of my phantoms ... I need
you still to give flesh to what goes on in my naked words ...

Listen listen to me a squirrel has just crouched on my
window sill ... schoolgirls and boys bloom in a shower of jokes
... restaurants welcome us with neon smiles ... airplanes
carry cargoes of illusions ... poems are born at the tips of
round breasts ... tomorrows sing somewhere among scuffles ...

'Life is grey she said show me some color.'
'Life is black he said show me a glint of light ...'

Nude bodies are cornucopia engendering all the grand
sarabandes ... and yet marsupial monsters pocket us in
public relations pouches: happiness comes in pills ... packages ...
props ... slops ... 'I vomit up my soul at the foot of a
streetlamp.' (What is there to do in this vale of tears
except cry): tautology ...

And yet your amianthus eyes oh my love are fireproof: liquid
glance spring tide of a new nativity in which desire to live
shines iridescent at last ...

– 'The sun is rising again' – she says.
– 'That's because the earth is still turning' – he says
   (stupidly)

1984

Translator's Afterword

Translator's Afterword

Here is a poet who is demanding, and therefore modest, lucid and therefore ironic, a poet who is inward-looking and therefore thunder-struck. JACQUES BRAULT

Gilles Hénault was born in Saint-Majorique, Québec in 1920, but raised in Montréal where his father worked for the Canadian Pacific Railway. With no formal instruction beyond high school, he remembers, 'When I really began spending time at the library – I was unemployed for a year or two – I had a chance to educate myself a little,' and this eventually led, when he was still in his teens, to work as a freelancer for the Montréal newspapers *Le Jour* and *Le Canada* and later, in the early forties, for *La Presse* and the news service of Radio Canada. His early poems appeared in *La Relève* and *La Nouvelle Relève* in 1940. By 1946, he was in the thick of cultural activity in Montréal: he founded a publishing house called *Cahiers de la file indienne* with his friend Eloi de Grandmont; he became closely associated with Paul-Emile Borduas and the group which was later called the Automatists; he joined the Communist Party and began writing for its newspaper, *Combat*. In fact, for a period of months in 1947, he was engaged in the fruitless task of trying to bring about some kind of mutual acceptance between readers and editors of *Combat* and the avant-garde artists of Montréal.

Hénault eventually left the Communist Party, discouraged by its stubbornly anglophone hierarchy and by policies that excluded Québec nationalists. But his continuing enthusiasm for the trade union movement led him to the textile strikes in Valleyfield in 1950 and eventually to Sudbury, Ontario, where he spent from 1952 to 1957 working for the miner's union as an organizer and as editor of their multi-lingual newspaper. After returning to Québec from Ontario in 1957, he supported himself with free-lance work in radio and television while writing and publishing poems. In 1959, he began a two-year stint as editor of the arts and letters page of *Le Devoir* and was also one of the founders of the important and very durable literary review, *Liberté*. His free-lance work in various media continued until 1966 when he became director of the Montréal Museum of Contemporary Art, a position he held for five years, mounting some of the first major exhibitions of Québec's non-figurative artists before returning to writing, teaching and translation. He won the Governor General's award for poetry in 1972 for *Signaux pour les Voyants* and later the Canada Council Prize for his translation of David Fennario's *Without a Parachute*. When not travelling, he has continued to live in Montréal.

Starting with experiments in traditional poetic forms, Hénault eventually turned to the French Surrealists for alternative models, especially to that branch of Surrealist-oriented writers who left the movement in the thirties essentially because of their pro-Communist leanings: Louis Aragon, Paul Eluard and others. His poem in memory of Eluard ends with the lines, 'Ta main nous tend / La clef des chants,' punning on *champs* (fields) and *chants* (songs). Someone who hands you 'la clef des champs' is proffering a key to the open fields; the key to your freedom. If we receive a musical clef as well, a 'key of songs,' we're doubly blessed. My point is that these two lines are a beautifully concise expression of admiration for one of the great musicians of modern love poetry, and also for a politically engaged writer. It is no accident that Hénault's poems, especially in the fifties and sixties, show some of the same qualities as Eluard's.

But this is a poet suspicious of language, who writes lines such as 'Hands know much more / than words' or 'Complex and unified life gets totally distorted, reflected in the glass of language.' Words are dangerous when they subvert freedom at the service of propaganda or advertising or mindless habit. For that reason they must be constantly questioned, or tricked:

> It is through movement and rhythm that the irrational crops up in the rational. But the rational is thereby transposed. It becomes a new language, to be learned anew, opened up. Semaphore, signals trapped by the radar of a new sensibility, a password to be decoded, a grille that lets through aberrant forms of the real, aberrant because we were so comfortable in our little mundane geometry of the known, in that masonry of words that seemed as if it would resist forever the black tide of the informal, the unformulated ...

Unlike the Automatist poet Claude Gauvreau, Hénault has not spent much time on linguistic experiments in his poetry, though he accepts experimental and formalist poetry as a necessary antidote to cliché, part of the on-going dialectic of subject and form. His own search is more for a 'poor' language 'connected to popular forms that are accessible and proverbial, but full at the same time; that provide all the dimensions of language; that are poor without being impoverished, transmitting experience at as high a level as possible, but presented as simply as can be.' And so, when we see him writing in *Sémaphore* what is perhaps the first semiotic love poetry in Canadian literature, it would be a mistake to pin labels such as post-modernist or deconstructionist on Hénault. A little poem entitled *Ecrits vains* (another pun I can only half catch), published in *Chroniques* in 1975, will set the record straight:

WRITE ERRS

Writing erases reality
   bakes new pie in sky
machination
   spatial illusion
      reflection
distorted
   reading between the lines
[nadanadanadanadanadanadanadanada]
nought
   'The pen mightier than the sword'
Hee-Haw!
   Essay the sword.
Seated snugly
   watching television
I write calmly
   the word revolution
'Mr. Clean, Mr. Clean, Mr. Clean'
   brains washed
Whiter than white ... To write
   just word-play.
What will we hear from the critic?
   tic tic tic tic ...
The pollution of sense
The senses of pollution
Essence of pollution
Pollution by essences

Come on, get serious
   mind pollutes sense
says the cri-tic-tic-tic-tic
   Note how the crazy cont
(ext) of the signified-signifiers
   subverts the structures
of the phrase (write-errs)
Text con-text pre-text anything goes
   come the revolution.
Goddamned language
   lone hedge
      against inflation

Wrestling with symbols
    opposing write to wrong
monomania mythomaniac
    shaman's song
        scrivanity
    inanity.

Nota bene: once you leave the text
    you're out in the street.

MEMBER OF THE SCABRINI GROUP

Quebec, Canada
2000